children first

children first

a celebration of children
by **TOP PHOTOGRAPHERS**
and **RECORDING ARTISTS**

A BULFINCH PRESS BOOK

Little, Brown and Company

BOSTON · NEW YORK · TORONTO · LONDON

FIRST EDITION
ISBN 0-8212-2355-0
LIBRARY OF CONGRESS CATALOG CARD NUMBER 98-73327

Bulfinch Press is an imprint and trademark of Little, Brown
and Company (Inc.)

Published simultaneously in Canada by Little, Brown &
Company (Canada) Limited

BOOK DESIGN: PETRULA VRONTIKIS,
VRONTIKIS DESIGN OFFICE, LOS ANGELES

PRINTED IN HONG KONG

SINCE ITS INCEPTION IN 1986, HOMES FOR THE HOMELESS HAS SERVED MORE THAN 9,600 HOMELESS FAMILIES AND 21,300

HOMELESS CHILDREN. THE DONATION YOU HAVE MADE BY PURCHASING *Children First: A Celebration of Children by Top*

Photographers and Recording Artists WILL ALLOW THEM TO CONTINUE TO DEVELOP CREATIVE STRATEGIES FOR BATTLING THE

EFFECTS OF HOMELESSNESS AND URBAN POVERTY ON THE LIVES OF CHILDREN AND THEIR FAMILIES. • TODAY, THERE ARE

APPROXIMATELY 2.3 MILLION HOMELESS CHILDREN IN AMERICA. THAT IS UNACCEPTABLE IN A COUNTRY THAT BOASTS OF BEING

THE GREATEST NATION ON THE PLANET. THE CHILDREN OF OUR COUNTRY ARE OUR FUTURE, AND AS WE APPROACH THE TWENTY-

FIRST CENTURY, WE CAN'T AFFORD TO LET THEM GROW UP WITHOUT THE SKILLS NECESSARY TO SURVIVE IN THE NEW CENTURY.

IF WE DO, THE END RESULT WILL BE CONTINUED GROWTH OF THE HOMELESS COMMUNITY. • WITH A PHILOSOPHY THAT

EDUCATION IS THE KEY TO BREAKING THE CYCLE OF HOMELESSNESS AND POVERTY, HOMES FOR THE HOMELESS AND THE

PROGRAMS THAT THEY HAVE DEVELOPED ARE NOT ONLY SUCCESSFUL IN ENDING THIS HORRIFIC CYCLE OF HOMELESSNESS, BUT

IN BREAKING THE CYCLE OF DEPENDENCY AS WELL.

QUINCY JONES

On the following pages, you will see a picture of children from all over the world—some are homeless; some are not. As you look at their faces, you will probably see no difference. All children share similarities—they all have fears, joys, and aspirations. But for an increasing number of children, one very real fear is that they and their parents will not find a home.

When asked to describe the homeless, most people talk about "bums" living on the streets, in the parks, and under the bridges of major cities. While this may have been true in the 1960s and '70s, today it is young families—*children and their mothers*—who are the fastest-growing segment of the homeless population. In fact, the average age of a homeless person is only *nine.*

These young families face a host of problems—including welfare dependency, family breakup, and lack of education. Housing alone cannot be the answer. At Homes for the Homeless, we quickly recognized that homelessness was an issue of children, of families, and of severe poverty. To have an impact, a much more comprehensive response was necessary— one that attacked homelessness at its roots.

We developed American Family Inns to do just that. In these residential facilities, young families receive the education, job training, and support they need to take their first steps toward independence. Each day, in four American Family Inns in New York City, we help more than 530 mothers and 1,000 children develop the skills, knowledge, and commitment to move from a world of hopelessness and welfare dependency to one of promise and independence. At the same time, our development of innovative education-based programs and experimentation with new ideas work to stimulate debate, foster new thinking, and encourage welfare reform initiatives on the national level.

As you look through this book, you may be reminded of the children in your life. Like all young children, the ones pictured here have hopes and plans for bright futures. Yet, to recall the words of President Johnson over thirty years ago, "You don't know the damage poverty can do until you see the scars it can leave on the face of a child who once had a dream." Our goal is to heal the scars and restore the dreams of millions of children for years to come.

RALPH NUNEZ
President Homes for the Homeless

PHOTOGRAPHY: ANDREA STERN

boys choir of harlem

Children believe they have a voice

and with that voice

make people listen.

When people listen

they acknowledge that child's existence.

That child understands

they're connected

one by one

to a larger picture.

That child has the voice

to change the world.

DAVID **BARTOLOMI**

Three American Indian Kids

What caught my eye was the late afternoon sun striking the silver metal disks on their headbands. The kids nodded side to side and up and down, playing with the light. Awaiting their turn to perform at a tribal dance competition, these three American Indian children in Omak, Washington, were enthralled with the light, having fun, beaming it in my direction.

I don't know if that unadulterated joy of having fun as a kid is what comes through in the photo, but that's what I was feeling when I took it. What moves me when I look at the picture now is the strength these kids possess; they are not just having fun, they are playing with the power of the sun.

PETER SERLING

For me, this interplay between innocence and power strikes a deep chord. It is easy to mythologize the innocence of kids as pure and simple, but kids, like adults, struggle (sometimes against incredible odds) with gaining a sense of control in their lives.

PATRICK
MCMULLAN

TROY
WORD

I remember my kindergarten teacher was named Nancy Drew.

I remember the smell of rubber tires from the school playground. I remember my father pushing my two wheeler up a hill. I remember eating watermelon under the kitchen table.

I remember swimming lessons at Lake Champlain, And the cold, dark water. I remember buying fudgsicles with my milk money. I remember all our babysitters were girls.

I remember red strawberries growing in our backyard, and green tomatoes. I remember wild blackberries from the woods that gave me a rash.

I remember picking fat worms off the driveway when it rained. I remember having chicken pox.

I remember our station wagon that smelled like metal. I remember my friend's pet rabbits and her above-ground pool.

I remember hanging upsidedown from trees. I remember our house was painted light green, and our next door neighbor was named Betty.

GRACE H U A N G

STEFANO
AZARIO

10

CLEO **SULLIVAN**

Copsa-Mica, Romania (1990)

DAVID STORK

I DON'T KNOW WHY THE KIDS LOOKED BACK. BUT IT IS IN LOOKING BACK THAT THEY IDENTIFY THE SOURCE OF THE BLACKNESS THAT SURROUNDS THEM: THE CARBON-BLACK FACTORY IN THE TOWN OF COPSA-MICA.

DRIVING INTO THIS TOWN WAS A RIDE INTO A MONOCHROME HELL. HILLY GREENS AND GYPSY REDS BECAME GRAY AND THEN BLACK. THE CARBON-BLACK FACTORY, WHICH HAD SPEWED FORTH THE CHARCOAL MIST, COATED THE TOWN WITH THE COLOR THAT BECAME THE PALETTE SYMBOL FOR THE DARK ERA OF CEAUSESCU'S REIGN. NICOLAE CEAUSESCU HAD BEEN THE MAD DICTATOR OF ROMANIA SINCE 1965, UNTIL HE WAS OVERTHROWN IN DECEMBER 1989. HE WAS EXECUTED ON CHRISTMAS DAY. *"THE DEATH OF THE ANTICHRIST," SAID ONE.*

THE CHILDREN HAD BEEN PLAYING IN THE FIELDS AND WERE DIRTY FROM THE POLLUTION THAT ENVELOPED THEM. THEY WERE PROBABLY KILLING THEMSELVES SLOWLY WITH RESIDUAL CHEMICALS AND CON-TAMINATED DRINKING WATER. I REMEMBERED MY OWN CHILDHOOD AND HOW I USED TO PLAY IN THE STREET WHOSE ONLY THREAT WAS THE SLOWLY PASSING CARS. *POTENTIAL KILLERS WERE VISIBLE TO ME.*

THE HEART AND SOUL OF ROMANIA HAD SUFFERED SO MUCH OVER THE YEARS UNDER THE RULE OF THE DICTATOR THAT THIS IMAGE CAME TO SYMBOLIZE THE PAST, PRESENT, AND FUTURE OF THE LIVING GENERATIONS IN THE COUNTRY. *ALL WERE EQUALLY BLEAK.*

I WOULD SPEND MUCH MORE TIME WITH THE CHILDREN OF ROMANIA IN THE FUTURE. AIDS BABIES, GYPSY CLANS, AND THE STREET KIDS OF BUCHAREST WOULD BE PHOTOGRAPHIC SUBJECTS. NONE OF THEM MADE ME THINK THAT CHILDHOOD WAS A HAPPY TIME.

INNOCENCE WAS LOST AT BIRTH

FOR MOST OF THESE CHILDREN.

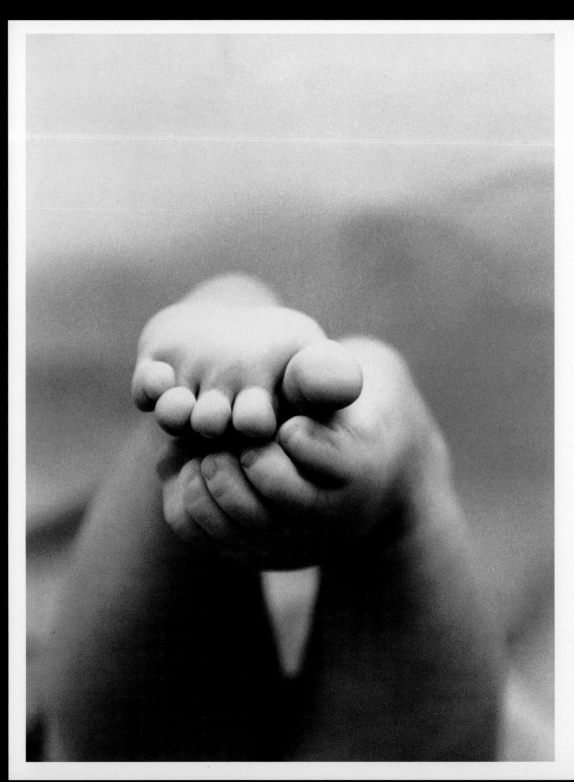

PETER
DAVIDIAN

FEETSOARING

INTO GIANT CLOUDS

PUSHING UP FROM UNKNOWN GROUND

INNOCENT. MATURE

MOVING THROUGH A HAZY VEIL

AN ALMOST

GREY, NEUTRAL

A SAFE
PLACE
A SAFE
PLACE

TO BE NURTURED AND GROW

A MIRACLE

A GIFT.

SHERYL NIELDS

15

Listen

What I heard my whole life
growing up is

Children should be seen and not
heard

What I'd like to start hearing
is people Listening!

SHE is speaking

LIZZIE **HIMMEL**

LISE
METZGER

ROBERT FLEISCHAUER

I was sitting on the beach, and this
boy was playing to the side of me. He was
all over the place like a bumblebee. I ran
back to the hotel for my camera, and he
was still lost in a fantasy world when
I returned. I got lost with him.
    Its that innocence, the purity of direction —
this way and that, bobbing and weaving —
who knows? who cares? lets play!
    I cherish it.

ANTHONY **GORDON**

PETER DAVIDIAN

CHRISTINA GALLAND

PRAYER

Mother of the crucified joker
wild wandering thin-faced man
Mother of love and lacerating life
the breath of cool sea winds
to soothe a hell burned sinner.
– I don't believe in Hell.
Mother of nature and all timid
easy prayers – for the God, the big one
we fear him most
and you are calm anti-mad woman,
of course, freak virgin mother
of freak thorn-crowned dead raiser
and wine maker and storyteller.

You break my heart with your sober beauty, so polite, so full of strange,
unreasonable grace and naive understanding which accepts even the
grimy dirt beggars from Lower East Side Sidewalk corners who (I must
be honest) I would never touch – yes look at out of curiosity.
I wish I could see with your eyes,
and taste with your unkissed, unsucked tongue,
oh pure mother of naked starving beautiful Jesus.
Take care of Christopher, we miss him. He's gone from us in a way
that's easy to know him. No warm skin no longer. He's gone like a
burned out flame, but I love him, and let my eyes be torn out by
vultures claws if I forget him.

Oh Mary, mother of God
and lovely holy human race
– creatures so powerful
they might destroy us all.
Mother of innocent ones,
prayer for evil ones,
singer of lullabies
and lover of all restless men
and cooker and cleaner
suppressed female of male dominant society
wrapped in an apron
cursing the hot frying pan
before cooking dinner.
I love you.

You break my heart with your silent sobs you try to hide from the world –
though you cry for the world, for all – for the half killed off living
remains families (Peter, a father, was killed by a cab) and even hungry
pathetic thieves and killers who never suffer for their inflicted harm.
You break my heart with your braveness to give birth to such a
madman - wild humorous joyous magician of the carnival.
You were brave Mary, you were brave.
And to watch him live and die – your son, the so full of life savior, like
my mother watched Chris – so full of life and love – die.
You were strong, oh good mother, you were strong.
You break my heart, when even after I've tortured you and lied and
cheated and prayed and was forgiven only to lie and cheat again – after
forgot my brother in heaven and forgot to pray - after I use you as a
symbol of art and humor and amusement – after all that you love and
embrace me, and you care about my petty worries and selfish tears.
You break my heart.
You break my heart.

JORDAN GALLAND

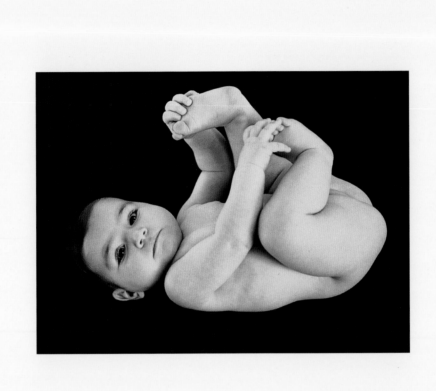

PETER **DAVIDIAN**

MAX
V A D U K U L

JON
GIPE

This photo was from a project
I shot for a homeless shelter
in Phoenix. The little girl and
her family had just moved into
temporary apartments provided by
the shelter. After working
on several homeless projects
I realized I had a very safe
childhood. I think any unloved
child is going to have many
problems. A lot of the
problems begin with the parents
who won't or can't take
responsibility because of substance
abuse or mental illness. There
are programs for people who
want to get off the streets and
I've found those with families
are much more likely to use these
resources.

JOAN
A L M O N D

PAMELA **HANSON**

DAVID J. PEREZ

KATRIN THOMAS

STEVE
HIETT

All children

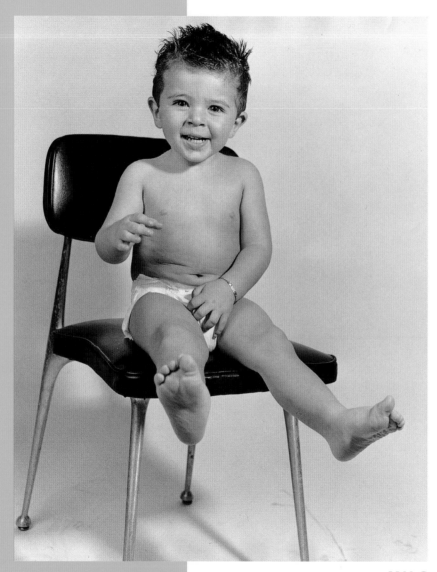

MILS

ARE beautiful

When they ARE brought into this
world they should be given the
same chances to grow up like the
chance I had when I was a child.

My childhood was filled with All
the good things that life had to
offer a child growing up in the
wilderness of Australia, being a free
spirit, just like in the photo of
"Roco" he represents that to me
full of wisdom + joy!

FRANK SITEMAN

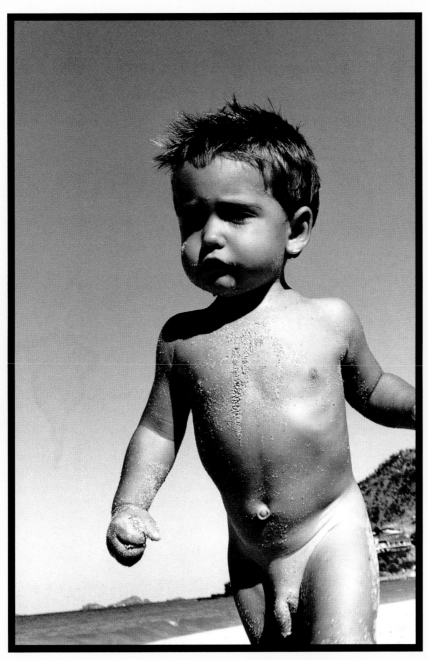

ANTOINE **VERGLAS**

JOAN
ALMOND

44

ROY
SCHATT

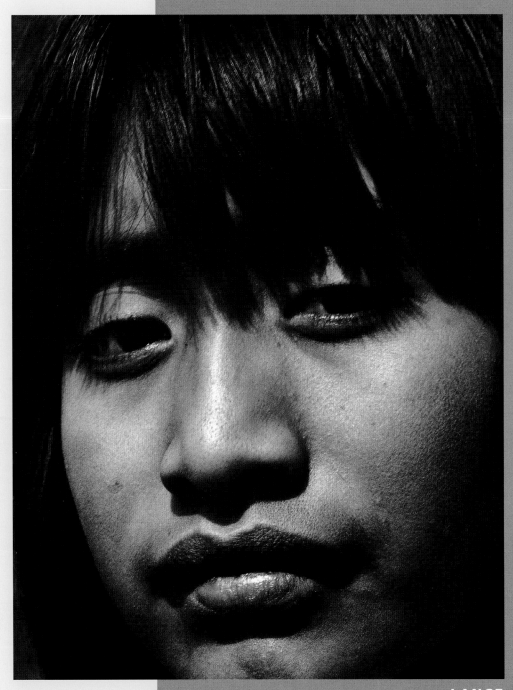

LANCE STAEDLER

- This photo was Taken in
The South of mexico 1991
The child is a Zapoteca
mexican indian.
- I felt she had a beautiful
face.
- When I was a child I always
wanted to be older
- I feel children today are
learning faster Than They
Were 50 years ago

Lauren

KAREN
MAINI

We had immediately bonded when I had met her the summer before,
but now that she was four and so verbal and mischievous,
we were bound for adventures. Her spirit was my muse
as I captured her on film and tape.

To me, she is all hope and light in this photograph.
The embodiment of hope — moving from the darkness into the light.
A child's innocence plainly shows us what is important in life.

MEI
T A O

ANTHONY CARONIA

"Jesus and I"

On a sunny September day in Central Park N.Y.C. I spotted
this boy taking a huge picture of a man for a walk who
sported long hair and a beard, but was not an alternative
rock star. The youthful image was a phantom-portrait of
the man who is worshipped by a large percentage of the
worlds population as a god and the son of god even though
he made very clear that he was not the only offspring.
Rather we are all children of god which makes us all
gods. That leaves us with a lot of responsibility.

Since there is so much effort and money invested into the
worship of this one particular Son, it seems amazing that
so many children of the present still have to suffer, still
are being neglected and need our attention.
Societies should be measured by the way they treat their
minorities. Children are a mute minority.
Jesus we still have a long way to go.

MANFRED GESTRICH

ANDREA STERN

Child hood shoued be a

PEGGY
SIROTA

time of creativity and hope.

Sharene is 11 years old, and regularly comes to the adventure playground. We found her standing among these cut-out figures, almost as though she was one of them. She seemed lost in her own world... We loved her smile, and the way the light plays on her and the surroundings.

ANDERSON & LOW

CHILDREN ARE POWERFUL BEINGS. THEY POSSESS SO MUCH

INNOCENCE AND HOPE. THERE ARE TIMES WHEN THE FUTURE

SEEMS UTTERLY FRIGHTENING. I THINK OF MY KIDS WHEN I

THINK OF THE FUTURE. KIDS ARE THE FUTURE. WHEN I

GET TOO FRIGHTENED, I THINK OF THE GREATNESS EACH CHILD

POSSESSES. IT HELPS.

WILLIAM ABRANOWICZ

DEBORAH **LOPEZ**

MICHAEL **TAMARRO**

KEN
SCHLES

WHEN WE TALK ABOUT CHILDREN

IN THE ABSTRACT WE ARE REALLY

TALKING ABOUT OURSELVES —

OF OUR HOPE AND THE POTENTIAL

FOR OUR OWN LIVED LIVES.

❧

THROUGH CHILDREN WE CAN

ELIMINATE THE REGRETS

OF THE WORLD.

KEVIN
SWEENEY

A Child

Have you noticed that every child runs,
    apparently for no reason;
    and yet I see the reason;
    they run with violence, chaos and frenzy;

        They run with a purpose,
            to go faster and faster;
            to run as if to stop time;
            to run so as to reveal the lie;

    So as to laugh at God, so as to be with Him;
    So as to defy hunger, so they may suffer starvation;
    So as to exist in the Paradox, so as to not;
    So as to love man with his dirty hands and silly wars,

        To run with conviction, yet no bearing;
        To have nowhere to run and yet to run to stop time;

        This is their power, let us remember, lest we forget;

And yet they will always come,
certain of stopping time,
smirking with defiance at our folly.
        Lest we not forget the children

EREZ S A B A G

NADAV
KANDER

ANA
N A N C E

To be a child is a gift, don't take that away.

Carefree laughter,
          playful joy.

                              Tricks and treats.

The potential to be damaged by experience or molded by fear.
The child will stay within all of us.
The child will tell the truth or hold the lie.
                              They will suffer tomorrow

            We are the future
We are responsible

SYBILLE CASTELAIN

DANIELA FEDERICI

74

FRANCESCO
SCAVULLO

STEVEN **KLEIN**

CHRISTIAN WITKIN

LIVES STRUNG ACROSS THEIR
WITH THEIR GOLDEN BODIES
AT THE WATERS EDGE, IT W
THIS CHILD THAT
A THOUSAND WOR
YOUNG AND WISE
THAT SPECIAL MO
AND BETWEEN

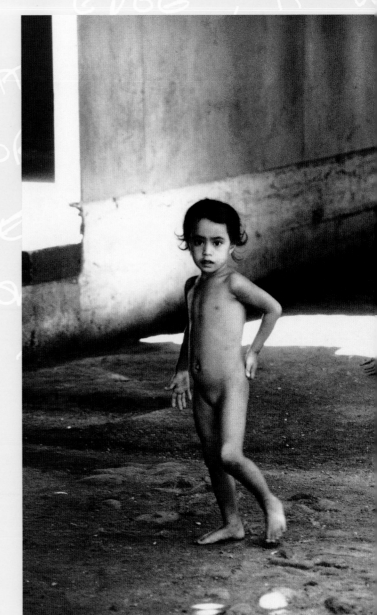

STEPHANIE **PFRIENDER**

WHILE TRAVELING THROUGH FRENCH POLYNESIA THE
ISLAND THAT CAPTIVATED ME FOR ITS SHEER NATURAL
BEAUTY WAS BORA BORA. THE BEAUTY CARRIED THROUGH
THE EYES OF THE CHILDREN, THEY ROAMED SO FREELY
QUITE OFTEN WITH A CLOTH OF BRIGHTLY COLORED
HUES STRUNG ACROSS THEIR TINY WAISTS OR NAKED
WITH THEIR GOLDEN BODIES TOUCHING THE PALMS
AT THE WATERS EDGE, IT WAS SIMPLE HAPPY LIVING.
THIS CHILD THAT I PHOTOGRAPHED SEEMED TO SAY
A THOUSAND WORDS THROUGH HER DARK EYES SO
YOUNG AND WISE THAT CAME TO MY CAMERA, IT WAS
THAT SPECIAL MOMENT OF A NATURAL CONNECTION TO
AND BETWEEN TWO PEOPLE.

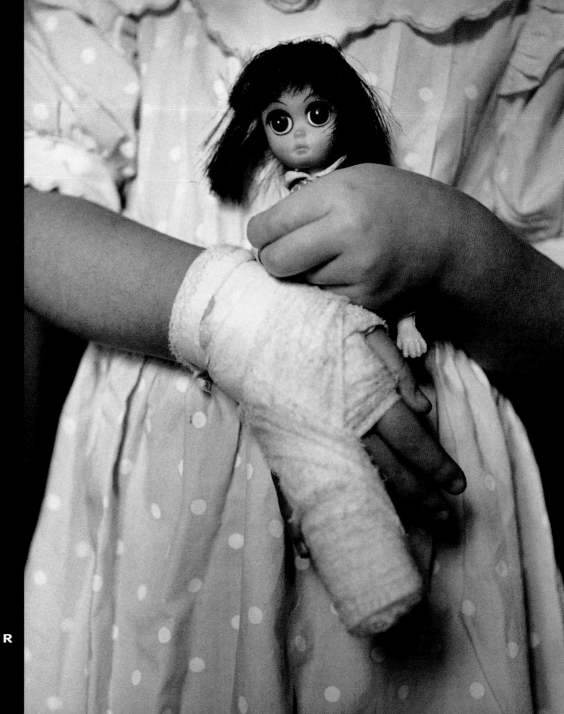

CEDRIC **BUCHET**

GERALD DEARING

JONATHAN
W E S T

JOSH
SHORE

I went to The Concourse House shelter in the North Bronx to visit with mothers and their children. Sitting in during the recreation period, I settled at a table to draw with a bunch of adorable little kids — all of them homeless. Eon, a six-year-old imp, beamed at me from afar, eventually mustering up the courage to edge his way over. Eon said nothing but took my pen, communicating with body language and pictures, not words.

I asked him if he could draw the sun. Confident, he delved into his craft, producing a beaming, brilliant sunshine, complete with a smiley face and long, stringy rays. Next, I asked him to draw a picture of himself. Instead of drawing the standard stick figure, he drew a page full of hearts (at least that's what his twin brother said they were). Then I suggested he draw a house. At first, this elicited no response. "A house," I repeated when he didn't seem to register. Finally he started into his picture, scribbling swirls, aimlessly. "A house," I said again. "Can you do that, Eon? Can you draw me a house?" Despite the row of houses outside the window — all other people's homes — Eon had no frame of reference, no experience from which to draw. Eon didn't have a house outside that window. So he just kept on scribbling...silent...no evidence of sadness, envy, embitterment, resentment. Eon's silent scribbling said it all.

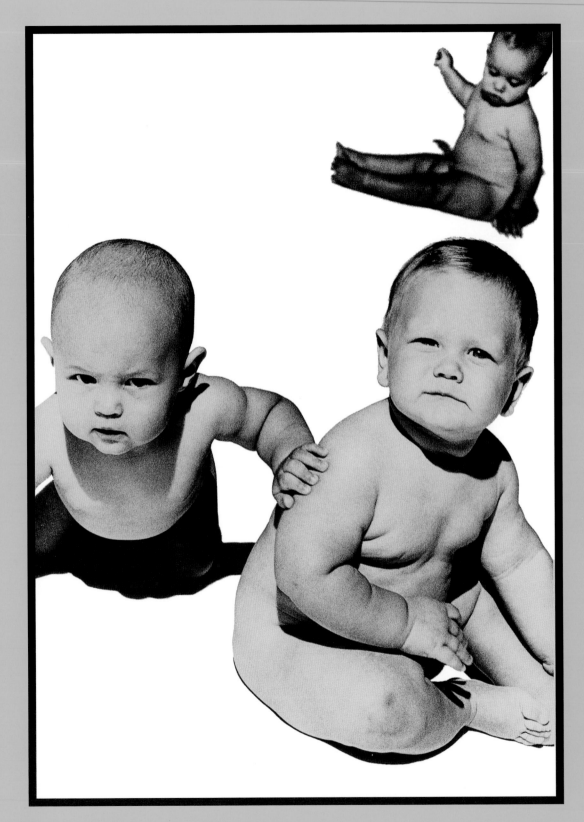

ARTHUR
ELGORT

SPRAGUE
HOLLANDER

CHILDREN MAKE US. IMMORTAL.

Acknowledgments

When Toneya Bird and Boss Models first approached me about this project I was somewhat awed by the difficulties inherent in pulling so many diverse elements together. It would have been a lot easier to just let their proposal get buried under the piles of papers that make my desk look like a war zone. But there was something so pure and so simple in what the essence of the *Children First* project encompassed that I knew from the first that the artists and employees of Reprise Records would want us to get involved. Everyone at Reprise is very proud to have been involved in bringing this project to life. I want to acknowledge especially the men and women who worked hard on their own time to help make sure our artists' musical efforts were part of this undertaking. First and foremost, hats go off to Dan Nathanson, who, in the end, never lost sight of the goal and never wavered in his dedication to seeing the *Children First* project through to the end. Without Dan's persistence and energy there would be no music in this book. Likewise I want to acknowledge the efforts above and beyond the call of duty from Rich Fitzgerald, Craig Kostich, Ilene Sutter, Julie Larson, Freddie DeMann, Rob Dickins, Carl Scott, Steve Lau, Jim Ed Norman, Gary Briggs, Max Hole, Daniel Miller, Jonathan Kessler, Elliot Roberts, Sheryl Louis, Howard Kaufman, Pete Fisher, Vincent Corry, José Quintana, Gary St. Clair, Marcie Webber, Barry Taylor, Billy Sammeth, Larry Wanagas, Steve Macklam, Sam Feldman, Tammy McCrary, Benny Medina, Roger Forrester, and of course, the generous musicians, producers, and engineers who donated their talent and energy to this endeavor.

HOWIE KLEIN

PRESIDENT   REPRISE RECORDS

Acknowledgments

Toneya Bird's passion for this project and her persuasive efforts on its behalf made this book happen. Boss Models is proud to represent Toneya; she is a rare and extraordinary beauty. Toneya was the motivating factor behind our participation in *Children First* and its unique format, since it was a very short time after her first visit to Homes for the Homeless that the concept of this book was born. I couldn't help but be swept up in Toneya's enthusiasm for the work of Homes for the Homeless and her desire to do something special for the organization. Toneya's tenacity and diplomatic skills made sure all the elements of *Children First* connected and each participant lent his or her expertise. Boss Models New York contacted the talented photographers whose work you see in this book and collected photographs from them for publication. The photographers were generous with their prints and waited patiently for this project to come to fruition. I would also like to thank Bulfinch Press, Reprise Records, Bob Perlstein, Paul West, and the staff of Boss Models Worldwide for bringing all the pieces together in this special package. The talents of so many have been given to this project, making it rich in spirit and beauty—a perfect reflection of the work of Toneya Bird for the cause of Homes for the Homeless and the organization's work on behalf of homeless families.

DAVID BOSMAN

PRESIDENT BOSS MODELS WORLDWIDE

ILLUSTRATION CREDITS

Italic indicates the pages on which photographs appear.

ANDREA STERN

children first

a celebration of children
by **TOP PHOTOGRAPHERS**
and **RECORDING ARTISTS**

CD CREDITS

1 **ERIC CLAPTON** "Motherless Child" 2:57

(Copyright information unavailable at date of printing) Produced by Eric Clapton and Russ Titelman. From the album *From the Cradle* (4/2-45735) ℗ 1996 Reprise Records.

2 **ME'SHELL NDEGÉOCELLO** "God Shiva" 4:08

(Music: Me'Shell Ndegéocello/Wendy Melvoin) Revolutionary Jazz Giant/Nomad Noman Music administered by Warner-Tamerlane Publishing Corp. BMI/Girl Brothers Music administered by EMI Virgin Music Inc. Produced by David Hiram Gamson. Arranged by David Hiram Gamson and Me'Shell Ndegéocello. Vocals arranged by David Hiram Gamson. From the album *Peace Beyond Passion* (2/4-46033) ℗ 1996 Maverick Recording Company.

3 **CHAKA KHAN** "Love Me Still" 3:28

(Chaka Khan/Bruce Hornsby) Chaka Khan Music/WB Music Corp./ Basically Zappo Music administered by WB Music Corp. ASCAP. Produced by David Gamson. Arranged by Bruce Hornsby. From the album *Epiphany: The Best of Chaka Khan* (2/4-45865) ℗ 1996 Reprise Records.

4 **JONI MITCHELL** "For Free" 4:31

(Composed and arranged by Joni Mitchell) © 1969 Siquomb Publishing Corp. BMI. From the album *Ladies of the Canyon* (2/M5G-6376) ℗ 1996 Reprise Records.

5 **HOLLY PALMER** "The Three of Us" 4:19

(Holly Palmer/Pete Glenister) Children of the Forest Music/Bug Butter Music BMI. All rights of Bug Butter Music administered by Children of the Forest Music BMI/Warner Chappell Music Ltd. PRS (administered by WB Music Corp. ASCAP). Produced by Kenny White and Holly Palmer. From the album *Holly Palmer* (2/4-46281) ℗ 1996 Reprise Records.

6 **CHER** "What About the Moonlight" 4:17

(Kathleen York/ Michael Dorian) WB Music Corp. ASCAP. Produced by Sam Ward for Elephant Music Productions. Original U.K. production by Christopher Neil. From the album *It's a Man's World* (2/4-46179) ℗ 1996 Reprise Records.

7 **BT** "Loving You More (BT's Final Spiritual Journey)" 3:29

(Vincent Covello/Brian Transeau) PolyGram Music UK PRS. Produced by Brian Transeau. From the album *Ima* (2/4-46356) ℗ 1996 Reprise Records.

8 **NU FLAVOR** "Heaven" 4:56

(R. Luna/F. Pangelinan/J. Ceniceros) BMI. Produced by Gary Sinclair for Hit Boy International. Associate producer: José Quintana. From the album *Nu Flavor* (2/4-46408 and 2/4-46410) ℗ 1996 Reprise Records.

9 **PAUL BRANDT** "I Meant to Do That" 3:28

(Lynn Gillespie Chater/Kerry Chater/Paul Brandt) Peermusic Ltd. ASCAP/Warner-Tamerlane Pub. Corp./ Pollywog Music SOCAN/BMI. Produced by Josh Leo. From the album *Calm Before the Storm* (2/4-46180) ℗ 1996 Reprise Records.

10 **CHRIS ISAAK** "Eyes of Texas" 2:06

(Chris Isaak) C. Isaak Music Publishing Co. ASCAP. Produced by Erik Jacobsen. ℗ 1996 Reprise Records.

11 **NEIL YOUNG WITH CRAZY HORSE** "Music Arcade" 3:59

(Neil Young) Silver Fiddle Music. ASCAP. Produced by Neil Young. From the album *Broken Arrow* (2/4/1-46291) ℗ 1996 Reprise Records.

12 **DEPECHE MODE** "Condemnation" 3:19

(Martin L. Gore) EMI Music Publishing Ltd. administered by EMI Blackwood Music Inc. BMI. Produced by Depeche Mode and Flood. From the album *Faith and Devotion* (2/4-45243) ℗ 1993 Sire Records Company.

Compilation produced by Howie Klein and Dan Nathanson

© 1997 Reprise Records. Made in U.S.A.
CD Photograph copyright © by Peter Davidian